LESLIE R. HERMAN

Anyone Can Meditate

How & Why to Begin A Guided Meditation Practice

First edition

This book was professionally typeset on Reedsy.
Find out more at reedsy.com

Contents

1

Introduction

Hello and Welcome to the introduction of this book, **Anyone Can Meditate.** Your guided meditation journey begins here!

My name is Leslie Herman. I am writing this book because I am passionate about guided meditation, and I'd like to share that with you. More than that I would like to inspire you to begin a guided meditation practice yourself, plus how and why to do so. If you've opened the book and begun reading, then that is a great start.

I was introduced to guided meditation in the 1980s, when I was a teenager and performing arts student. Our movement classes began with a warm-up and ended with a cool-down. A guided meditation was very often incorporated into the cool-down. I really enjoyed them. Then later on in my adult life, about 15 years ago, in around 2008, I began using guided meditations for more personal reasons. This was a time when guided meditation content was sparse, but thankfully there was enough to get started.

What content I did find, and how I benefited, was like striking gold, at a time in my life when it felt like I was mining for solutions and guidance and was only hitting on fool's gold. Guided meditations are golden nuggets and they have made me rich.

Meditation is a very personal experience. So don't worry, this book is not a prescription. My meditation experience is mine. Yours will be yours. I will not tell you what to do or how to do it. One of the main reasons I love this method of meditation is because it is most definitely not prescriptive, and once you get into the groove you can and will tailor your practice to your own needs. This is especially true today because there is so much content availableout there, you will have no problem accessing it and finding the guided meditations that are just right for you. I truly believe that anyone can meditate. And without *shoulding* all over the place, I do believe that everyone *should*. At the very least, I wish that everyone would try it and find out for themselves.

If you are interested in beginning to meditate and don't know where to start, guided meditation is the simplest and easiest way to begin. There are other, different ways of meditating, but the focus of the book is guided meditation.

In my opinion, as someone who has tried other ways and finally landed on guided meditation as my preferred way to meditate, and the way I have stuck with and benefited from, guided meditation is the method I celebrate for my own wins and recommend to others because of that.

By sharing my knowledge and passion in a book about this rich vein for relaxation, well-being, self-awareness and personal development, it is my intention to inspire more people to begin their own guided meditation practice. And if I can help make guided meditation more accessible by demystifying it for you, and making it easy for you to get started, then I have done my job.

I wish you well at the start of your guided meditation journey! Let's begin.

* * *

2

What is guided meditation?

Guided meditation is the method I celebrate for my own wins and recommend to others because of that.

If you are interested in beginning to meditate and don't know where to start, guided meditation is the simplest and easiest way to begin. Yes, there are other, different ways of meditating, but in my opinion, as someone who has tried other ways, like transcendental meditation, for example, I was so grateful to have found and stuck with guided meditation.

Guided meditation is just that. Someone else's voice is Your Guide. From the absolute beginning to the very end of the session, your guide is there to instruct, advise, and support you all the way.

Be assured. No extra pressure whatsoever is imposed upon you. It is understood that you've got enough on your plate. The last thing you want is a shopping list – must-spend on a must-wear uniform, or must-have gear, and a set of strict instructions on what to do. There are no must-haves, must-wears or must-spends with guided meditation. Once you have made a decision to try it, all you need is a bit of time, and then all you have to do is show up.

Oh! You might want a pair of headphones or earbuds. But don't worry if you don't have a pair, you can do guided meditation without them.

The primary reasons you might wish to wear headphones or earbuds are:-

- you will be able to listen to the guidance without the distraction of other noises around you that may be out of your control;
- you will be able to hear the guides more clearly;
- it may help your focus and help your flow while meditating.

If it's a toss up, meaning you could go either way, and you have the choice, I recommend you use them. You will be able to monitor how loud you are playing the guided meditation – with headphones on you are more likely to have it at a safe volume – and in the long term that is the safest for your hearing and ear health.

* * *

3

Where to go to do guided meditation

So, where do you show up? These days the most common place is wherever you are! You can tap into a guided meditation online, so wherever you are, a guided meditation is available. Go to YouTube, type in 'guided meditation', and a slew of content will become available to you. Later in the book I will give you suggestions about how to target your search to find one that meets your specific needs at any time. It is a given that, on a daily basis, your needs may change.

Don't worry – there is a guided meditation to meet your needs.

You may also find guided meditations that are offered in a group or classroom setting. Typically, a guided meditation is added on to the end of a yoga class or other movement classes. And I'm aware of bespoke guided meditation classes popping up more and more in the live space. This can be a very rewarding guided meditation experience, and a group guided meditation can be very powerful and serve a collective purpose beyond your own personal needs. If you are interested and can find one, go for it! But remember, you can only access a live guided meditation when and where they are offered. So, for the purposes of this book, I will focus on online guided meditation.

The beauty of online guided meditation content is that you can access it on demand, for free, and you can do it at any time and wherever you are.

* * *

4

Ready. Set. Wait! One more thing before you begin

What is Your Why?
Ask yourself, 'Why do I want to begin to meditate?' Ok, no pressure. I promised there would be no pressure. You don't have to, but, answering this question will be helpful before you begin. And some of you may already know 'your why'. And that's great.

'Your why' may simply be that you are curious. Maybe some of your friends are trying it, so you want to try it, too. Someone you respect and admire may have recommended it to you, so you feel it may be worth trying. Perhaps you are anxious or worried about something all the time, and you would like to feel less anxious or worried. There are as many whys as there are people in this world!

What is 'your why'? When you understand your why, the outcomes and benefits of meditation will become clearer. You will be able to recognise the changes that have occurred. For example, if 'your why' is for relaxation, then when you begin to feel more relaxed on a regular basis, or even possibly immediately after the meditation, you will be able to see clearly that the meditation has helped you to feel more relaxed. Here is another example, for more complex whys: Say you have a problem you need to solve, or a crisis you need to resolve. You set this as 'your why', and you do your guided meditations with this in your mind. You set it, then you forget it. You do not have to *think* about your why throughout. Your why is like a seed you have planted – the meditation will be the nourishment you give your why – and when you find the solution, or resolve the crisis, you will be able to acknowledge that the meditation has helped you to do so. I hope that makes sense!

* * *

5

Reasons to begin a meditation practice

1.Starting is easy. All you have to do is make the time for it.

2.Guided meditations are accessible. Wherever you are, and whenever the mood strikes you, you can tap into a guided meditation. For this reason it is great for beginners to start a meditation practice, and it is also the reason it is easy to keep a guided meditation going.

3. You will be supported. You are supported by a professional. From start to finish of the session, your guide is there to instruct, advise, and support you.

4.Timings are flexible. Guided meditations are as long or as short as you want. There are guided meditations as short as 3 minutes or as long as 8 hours, and everything in between – 10 minutes, 20 minutes, 1 hour, 2 hours, etc. It is your choice. You decide.

5. Guided meditations are multi-purpose. There are guided meditations available for so many varied reasons and purposes. I always find

something I can tune into to serve my purpose, my why.

6. There is no pressure. You are not expected to get results right away. Depending on your why and the complexity of your why, you may experience benefits right away, you may have to be patient. Give yourself and give the practice a chance. Everything new takes time to adjust to. Results will flow a lot better if you take the pressure off yourself, manage your expectations, and give guided meditation a fair chance.

7.You will benefit.You are almost guaranteed to gain some benefits if you make guided meditation a habit, stick with it, keep an open mind, and trust the process.

* * *

6

How to get started

Remember! Starting is easy.

Make time

All you have to do is make some time for it, and the great thing is you can start with 3 or 5 or 10 minutes.

Make time at night

My suggestion is to tune into a guided meditation when you get into bed and before you go to sleep. That way, starting your practice doesn't have to cut into other activities in your scheduled routine. As long as you are not exhausted and you won't fall asleep in 3 seconds after your head hits the pillow, then before you sleep is a great time to start. Ending your day with a short guided meditation can help you have a deep, restful sleep, too!

Make time in the morning

Another great time to begin or add to your time for meditation is upon waking up, and before you get out of bed. Once again this will not put a demand on your time or cut into your other activities. Starting your day with a short guided meditation is highly recommended.

Prepare the space

This will be so easy if you decide to meditate in bed – either before you go to sleep or when you wake up – or both. Your bed *is* your meditation space. What could be easier than that!

Most guides, when you choose a meditation, will give you some guidance on preparing the space. You will oftentimes hear them say things like:

'For best results please use headphones. Do not drive or operate heavy machinery. If you are indoors, let some fresh air into your room, or go outside, if the weather suits you. Find a comfortable space where you will not be disturbed. Sit down or lie down. Allow for your body to feel unrestricted by clothing or anything else. When you have found yourself in a comfortable position, gently close your eyes, and place your attention onto your breath...'

Your breath

Meditation begins when you begin to pay attention to your breath. People take breathing for granted, because we do it automatically, we don't have to think about it. So, when we begin to focus on our breath, and pay attention to the air going in, the air going out, it helps take your mind off yesterday and tomorrow, and you will begin to tune into being alive in that exact moment you are in – the here and now.

If you become distracted by racing thoughts, the dog barking, something you forgot to do earlier in the day, any stress, worries or other negative emotions, come back to the focus on your breath. You may hear your guide suggest this.

Focusing on your breath is like putting down an anchor —- it will have a noticeable effect on your mind and your body. Plus, it is something most of us can do with relative ease, so we are not afraid that it is something we cannot do.

As you focus on your breath you will be guided back to the present of the exact moment – the here and now. This may help you to begin to feel better. While focussing on your breath you will begin to breathe a bit slower and deeper, which allows more oxygen to flow into the bloodstream, and aids relaxation.

A square is always a rectangle but a rectangle is not always a square. Have you heard that before? I am reminded of that comment from geometry lessons when it comes to breathwork. Breathing is intrinsically connected to meditation. But you can do breathwork and not meditate. For the purposes of this book, where there is meditation, breathwork will always be mentioned and will be part of the practice.

Your why

Ask yourself the question, why do I want to meditate tonight? The answer will vary. It may change every day, or it may be the same for several days, weeks or months at a time. The same why's may recur on a rotating basis. The more you tap into your why the clearer it will become. I suggest you keep it real simple. Of course it is up to you – simple or complex – go for it, whichever way you wish. You will find a guided meditation to meet your why. If your why is a bit more complex, the exact why may not pop up immediately, so you may have to change the wording a bit until something close presents itself in the search.

Your why may be attached to an emotion:
I want to be happy. Or I feel sad. I feel angry. I feel empty.
It may be something related to your moods or your mental health:
I am lonely. I'm worried about something. I want to be more positive.
I want to have a great day.

It may be something physical:

16

I am so tired, I want to get a great night's sleep. I have a headache. I can't sleep. I have had a diagnosis and I wish to help myself get better. I have neck and shoulder pain.

It may be related to a problem, something that is going on in your life:
I want to find a way to make up with my best friend, or I want to get over the break up with my partner, or I want to improve my relationships.

Any 'why' is a valid 'why'. And there will be a guided meditation for you. You may want to remember your dreams. Or you may have a dream you wish to come true.

Wishing for your dreams to come true relates to a huge topic dealing with the law of attraction and manifestation. Meditation is closely linked to mindset. There are tons of guided meditations if you are interested in the law of attraction and manifestation.

Go to YouTube. Search 'Guided Meditation for'
Remember to use those words, **'guided meditation' in your search** or the search will not offer you guided meditations. It may be about the subject of your why, but I won't necessarily give you meditations for your why.

If you are going to be doing your meditation at the end of the day and/or before you sleep, then you might want to add the word, 'short', and search for **'short guided meditations for....'**

For each of the WHYS listed above, I give examples of what to search for below:

- Short Guided Meditation for a great night sleep
- Short Guided Meditation to start the day right
- Guided Meditation for happiness
- Guided Meditation for sadness
- Guided Meditation for anger
- Guided Meditation for emptiness
- Guided Meditation for loneliness
- Guided Meditation for worry, or maybe try
- Guided Meditation for anxiety
- Guided Meditation for positivity
- Guided Meditation for headaches
- Guided Meditation for insomnia, or maybe try
- Guided Meditation for restlessness
- Guided Meditation to heal my body, or maybe try
- Guided Meditation for physical healing
- Guided Meditation for neck and shoulder pain
- Guided Meditation for conflict resolution, or maybe try something like
- Guided Meditation on how to apologize
- Guided Meditation for breakups
- Guided Meditation for relationships

Remember, these are just a few examples. Follow your why. Your why will guide you to the most relevant guided meditation. Once you begin searching, you will see just how much content is available to you for free. And the more you do it the more complex your whys may become and the better you will get at tweaking your keyword search to get amazingly close to your why. All of this will deepen and broaden the meditations that are presented to you.

How will you know which ones are right?

Later on in the book I will give you some of my personal recommendations. Before long you will have your list of personal favorites.

Trust your head

There will be voices that appeal to you more than others. That is ok. It is your choice. If you don't like something for whatever reason, switch it off and try another. There is plenty to choose from. Find the voice that feels right for you.

Trust your heart

You might listen to someone once and you won't like what they are saying. It might be clear right away to you or it may be halfway through. That is ok. In that case, switch it off. Choose another one. It may take a few times before you find one you can settle with. That is ok.

Trust your gut

If you are not sure but you are getting some kind of sensation – or message – maybe a sense in your head, your ears, your heart, or your gut that this guided meditation does not feel right for you. For whatever reason, trust that. Switch it off. That is your intuition. That sensation from wherever it comes is a message that it's not for you. That is ok.

Once you find the voices and messages that are right for you, you will feel as though you have a connection with your chosen guides. They are your ally, your buddy, your friend. They are here for you. They want to help you to be the best person you can be. You trust them. You appreciate them. Your guided meditation guides are new tools in your well-being tool box.

* * *

7

The benefits of meditation

So what are the benefits of meditation? Everybody is different. Everyone responds to things differently and at different speeds. How people respond to meditation is no different. Everyone will achieve different levels of wellness and within different timeframes. As long as you are aware of this, you can manage your expectations.

As your meditation practice becomes part of your daily routine, you will be able to gauge how it is going for you. You will be the best judge of this, so it is entirely up to you.

Tracking your meditation progress

If you are really, truly interested in monitoring your progress through your meditation journey, the best thing you can do is keep a meditation journal. Tracking your progress in a journal can be as short and simple as writing a single word before you begin each session and a single word when your session ends. Or it can be as lengthy and complex as you want it to be. The one word or shorter entries can be easier to monitor over a longer period of time. The word can be absolutely anything that resonates with you at the time. Oftentimes it will be a word that links to your why.

There is a lot of scientific research being done now on the benefits of meditation. More, detailed information can be found online or in the library. Here is an snapshot of how you may benefit, in no particular order, including in the short and long term – physically, emotionally, mentally and spiritually:-

- Gives deep rest to the entire body
- Enhances relaxation
- Improves quality of sleep
- Calms the nervous system
- Reduces fear of insomnia
- Enables proper rest
- Facilitates stress management
- Decreases anxiety
- Reduces depression
- Helps you feel happier
- Promotes self-improvement
- Improves self-awareness, intuition, self-confidence, self-trust, self love
- Increases empathy and compassion
- Enhances inner peace
- Helps build resilience and self sufficiency
- Increases enjoyment
- Appreciation of being alone and of silence
- Improves mental clarity, including memory
- Increases attention span and concentration
- Improves daily functioning and productivity
- Enhances creativity
- Increases cognitive ability

- Reduces cognitive rigidity
- Inspires critical thinking
- Aids in addiction recovery
- Aids in conflict resolution
- Supports improved relationships with others
- Facilitates pain management
- Facilitates heart health and reduces blood pressure
- Improves immune system functioning

Collective benefits

When you derive improvements and benefits, and when you feel better, you may want to begin to think about how you can participate in helping to create a better world. There is a strong belief in the collective benefits of meditation. When you meditate you can expand your why to include helping heal the world, creating world peace, inspiring solutions to climate change. This is something to look forward to when you are ready. Many guides include prayers and meditations towards the collective consciousness.

World Peace Meditation Day

Since 1986, December 31 is World Peace Meditation Day. On December 31, 1986 over

500 million people of all religious faith in over 70 countries joined their minds in peace,

love, forgiveness and understanding. The event is still going on, for one hour starting at

noon Greenwich Mean Time, with groups gathering in all U.S. states and around the world.

Also called World Healing Day or the International Hour for Peace, this simultaneous global

linking of minds takes as it's basis the principle of quantum physics that

thought can direct

energy, creating reality. Meditating on peace can create peace. Source: eocinstitute.org

* * *

8

Connect with the guides

Every guided meditation guide is different. Each one brings their own special qualities and unique styles to their guided meditations. Each one has their areas of specialization, too. In the beginning, it is suggested that you choose your guided meditations based on your why. Over time, you will find yourself drawn to your favorite guides, for your own reasons, and that will be another way of choosing a guided meditation on any given day.

I have been meditating using guided meditations for 15 years. There wasn't as much choice as there is today, and I am still endeared and indebted to the guides I discovered in the early days. Because the choice is an intuitive one, I still choose my guides the same way as when I first started. Here's how:

First, I am drawn to a guide's voice. I will make a holistic decision about their voice, which involves all my senses – it has to sound right but it also has to feel right. While I'm being drawn in by their voice, I'm also listening for their style – is it personal, is it formal, is it robotic, is it gentle, bossy? I have not got this on a checklist or anything like that but depending on my mood, and my particular needs, I figure out whether their style fits my needs. And finally, also very importantly, the actual messaging and content determines whether I will stay with the meditation or switch it off, and try another one. It has to be right or the meditation won't flow.

I personally love meditations that offer some explanation and some education. Not only are they teaching me something that I feel is valuable to know about, it helps me build trust that the guide knows their stuff.

Personal Favorites

These are just some of my personal favorite guides. As you can see by their YouTube subscriber numbers, I am not the only one who likes them!

Rasa Lukosiute Pura Rasa Guided Meditations @purarasa has 355K subscribers

This is a safe space where you will find various types of meditations; ranging from physical healing, sleep aid, law of attraction, deep relaxation, meditations to help strengthen your sixth sense and more. You will also find music, sounds of nature for sleep, relaxation and for your personal meditations. By using this meditation library you will find your centre, quiet your thoughts, relax deeply and feel grounded. This is the space where you will delve deeper into your subconscious to achieve lasting results. Through regular video uploads, I will provide you with as many effective tools as possible to live peacefully in the modern world. Subscribe and I will meet you in the next meditation! With appreciation, Rasa

Linda Hall Meditation @LindaHallguidedmeditation has 53.4K

subscribers

Meditations for relaxation and personal development with Linda Hall, inspirational meditation teacher and personal development coach. Linda's approach to meditation combines mind-body awareness and psychology with spirituality and does not align itself with a belief system or religion. Her experience spans thirty years in the integrative healthcare field; she is qualified in subtle energy healing, Clinical Hypnosis, N.L.P. Coaching and Emotional Freedom Technique and has been teaching meditation for over twenty years. Chronically ill with M.E./Chronic Fatigue Syndrome for almost a decade some years ago gave her first hand experience of the profound benefits of meditation. A warm and insightful teacher, Linda is passionate about enabling others to feel empowered through mindfulness and self-compassion. Her MP3s and CDs have found a global audience.

Jody Whiteley @jodywhiteley has 151K subscribers
For bedtime, naptime, relax time, or fun time.

Michael Sealey @MichaelSealey 1.79M subscribers227 videos

Hi, my name is Michael and welcome to my channel, where I hope you can stop by to relax, listen in, and see for yourself the power of positive hypnosis. Hypnosis is a completely natural state of often deeply felt relaxation and focused attention, where positive suggestions can be more easily accepted by our subconscious minds. Imagine a fantastic and tranquil state of daydreaming, and that is very close to hypnosis! Hypnosis can bring us improved self control, clearer and empowered behavioural choices, and allow us to listen to our best inner resources. Many people experience a deep sense of calmness and serenity during hypnotic meditation and are often pleasantly surprised to see the ongoing, life enhancing results. Thank you greatly for your support, feel free to subscribe and comment on your great results, and

I trust you will benefit from your time spent with positive hypnosis.

Jason Stephenson @jasonstephensonmeditation has 3.17M subscribers

I'm dedicated to sharing a '#peace' of my life with you! Through the use of #meditation, guided visualization, inspiring talks and relaxation music, you're about to open yourself to changes of immense harmony for your body, mind and spirit. jasonstephenson.net/lp/free-resources

Deepak Chopra The Chopra Well @TheChopraWell 617K subscribers

Welcome to The Chopra Well! Our channel is dedicated to inspiring, fun, and thought-provoking videos about healthy living, wellness, and spirituality. We are anchored by doctor and author Deepak Chopra, as well as family & friends, who hope to provide you with tools for personal and social transformation. We deal with some serious topics and themes here, but we definitely don't take ourselves too seriously either. We encourage you to watch a few videos, engage with us and fellow viewers by sharing comments, and subscribing to show your support for our channel. We have several new videos every week, so come back soon. Thanks for visiting and supporting our channel! Deepakchopra.com

Sara Raymond: The Mindful Movement has 775K subscribers

Thank your for visiting The Mindful Movement! Take a minute to get to know Sara and Les Raymond, the founders of the channel, and what the channel is all about. We founded The Mindful Movement in August of 2016 because we are passionate about helping others grow and live mindful, fulfilled lives. We have both experienced profound growth and fulfillment living a mindful lifestyle. Together we help others live a more mindful life, deepening their awareness and sense of gratitude. We strive to inspire others to live authentically with love and abundance.

We created this channel to offer powerful guided meditations, guided hypnosis, mindful movement practices and helpful mindful tips for you, to enhance the quality of your life in numerous and profound ways. Do not listen while driving. Meditation and mindful movement are powerful tools to support you. This is not a substitute for medical care. Consult a doctor or trusted health professional if needed.

Ally Boothroyd | Sarovara Yoga @SarovaraYoga has 176K subscribers
Ally Boothroyd is a Yoga Nidra educator & YTT facilitator, yoga educator & meditation teacher.

Sarah Dresser Unlock your Life @unlockyourlife has 375K subscribers
Welcome! My name is Sarah Dresser, Clinical Hypnotherapist, and I'm passionate about low cost and no cost therapy and support for all. I believe everyone deserves someone to support them in life. And I want everyone to benefit from the power that we all have in our mind to overcome even decades long issues. Here you'll hypnotherapy, meditations and affirmations for anxiety, stress, sleep, self-esteem and an exploration of our spiritual world. I write every script myself, combining the art of guided imagery, the latest research from fields within neuroscience and psychology, and combine all these with powerful transformative techniques from my clinical hypnotherapy training. I am also the creator of the original Think Yourself Slim Program which is a result of more than 10 years of research, and everything I've learned I've put into the most powerful weight loss hypnosis program ever! Allow me to support you to unlock your life, starting today. Always here to help, Sarah. thinkyourselfslim.com

Kenneth Soares@KennethSoaresUniverse has 147K subscribers

Dear Soul, Thank you for being here. I'm a Loving Soul who is here to learn, teach and Shine my Light. My Life Purpose is to spread practical Knowledge, Wisdom and Healing with Love and Enthusiasm - that Inspires and awakens people to their Greatness & Potential, and make this world a Peaceful, Joyful and Loving place for ALL Life. instagram.com/kennethsoares.livingfully

There are so many guided meditation guides to choose from. And these are just some of my personal favorites, though I am always seeking new voices and alternative delivery styles.

* * *

9

Sample guided meditations

Guided meditations are best when you listen to them, but I wanted to show you an example of a short one. I am confident that your why will take you on a journey of discovery to find the guided meditations that are right for you.

5-Minute Meditation You Can Do Anywhere

"Think of this next few minutes as a gift to yourself. Even just a few short minutes can have a positive impact on your day. So settle into a comfortable position, seated or lying down, then gently close your eyes, and focus all of your attention onto your breathing, taking deeper and slower breaths than you have all day so far. Take a deep breath in through your nose and slowly let it out through your mouth. Continue to breathe that way, feeling your lungs expand out as you inhale and contract back in as you exhale. Tune into your body; notice how it feels and if there is anything it is trying to tell you — are there any places in your body that are feeling tired, tense, tight, or a bit wobbly, or tied up in knots? give those areas permission to relax, send love into those areas and thank your body for taking such good care of you and let it know that it's ok to rest and relax for these next few minutes. You may

31

notice that your mind starts to wander off, that's ok; it's natural. Just notice it and bring your attention back to your body using your breath as your anchor. Try to picture one thing that's happened today that has made you smile or has made you thankful or appreciative and just let that feeling fill you up for a moment. Breathe that feeling in from the top of your head to the tips of your toes and allow yourself to smile if that feels natural. Now focus on something you can do today whether it's for yourself or for someone else that will allow you to continue feeling this way, it could be something like deciding to go to bed early tonight or the joy of telling someone special that you love them. What is one little thing that you can plan for your day that will bring you joy? Now sit in that feeling of joy and peace for a moment longer.... as you breathe slowly and deeply.... nothing else matters for now.... this is all that matters.... the joy and the peace of this moment. Now in your own time, when you're ready you can gently open your eyes and enjoy the rest of your day. " Source: Goodful@Goodful has 1.57M subscribers https://youtu.be/inpok4MKVLM?si=hFslaGXoZi3SOypr

One of my personal favorite guided meditations is the **HO'oPonoPono prayer**, delivered by Sandra Rolus.

Ho'oponopono is an ancient Hawaiian practice of forgiveness and reconciliation. Traditionally it was practiced by family members for a person who was physically ill as it was thought that guilt over errors the person had committed had made them sick. Modern researchers have found that the applications of Ho'opono pono can have far reaching implications and can be used in any situation, problem, issue, relationship or concern, simply by using your intention and attention to use these 4 key mantras for healing of all relationships and for manifestations of abundance and prosperity in all areas of your life. Dr. Ihaleakala Hew Len was a therapist at the Hawaii State Hospital. He worked with patients who had been diagnosed as dangerous and

SAMPLE GUIDED MEDITATIONS

criminally insane. When he began working there, the ward he was on was assigned to was not a good place to be. The staff including the doctors quit or called in sick on a regular basis. It was a high-stress environment with many staff terrified of the patients and we can say, it was just as bad for the patients as many of them were shackled or heavily sedated. As Dr. Hew Len would review a patient's file he would practice Ho'opono Pono repeating the key mantras over and over again and directing them not at the patients as you might have expected, but at himself as at the centre of Ho'opono Pono lies the belief that we all have a responsibility for the reality we experience. So, Dr. Hew Len believed that to heal these patients he would first have to heal himself and as he did so, incredibly, even patients he had never seen began to heal. Patients came off their medication, stopped being violent and some were even released. People began enjoying coming to work there and absenteeism and staff turnover stopped. Dr. Hew Len's story then began to circulate and as people began to practice this amazing, profound yet simple technique they began to see incredible changes take place in their lives as blockages to success, to happiness and wellbeing just seemed to disappear.

Ho'oponopono for Self Love & Radical Forgiveness Sandra Rolus has 168K subscribers

Today's guided sessions is all about Forgiveness and Self love
Repeat out loud these 4 simple phrases
I'm sorry
Please forgive me
Thank you
I love you
You will get the best result if you do this deep healing exercise 2x/day, in the morning before you start your day and right before you go to sleep.
https://youtu.be/QQTtoOBaypw?si=QHPiLJIoeefNGcEj

Music by Christopher Lloyd Clarke. Licensed by Enlightened Audio ::

I find this one very powerful and effective. I return to it over and over. What do you think? I'd love to know if you've tried and and how you found it. Check it out on YouTube.

If you are looking for more inspiration, please request to join the Facebook group, **Anyone Can Meditate**. Here you will find heaps of recommended guided meditations and more great content about meditating. Because of the personal nature of the subject, it is a private group. If you are interested, you can request to join. You will be welcomed. https://www.facebook.com/groups/1491000371266232

* * *

10

Anyone can meditate, honestly!

I hope this book has inspired you to begin to meditate using guided meditation. Just a final few words for the people who think that meditation is not for them or that they just can't do it. There is a famous inspirational saying that is credited to the founder of the Ford Motor Company, Henry Ford: *"One of the greatest discoveries a person makes, one of their great surprises, is to find they can do what they were afraid they couldn't do."* This is sometimes shortened to: *" If you think you can, you can; if you think you cannot, you cannot."*

It is a mindset thing. Resistance to something new is natural. Try a short one. Try a few different ones. Just give it a try. And remember there are virtually no rules, and you don't have to do much of anything to get started. Getting started with guided meditation is as easy as finding a comfortable spot and tuning in – then letting your guide do the work.

The only thing you have to do is keep an open mind. At the very least, the only thing that is asked of you is that you are receptive to the possibility that this simple practice may be something you will enjoy and benefit from.

And, you know what? If you are certain it is not for you, then that may be true for you right now. But remember, the door to guided meditation is always open. If it is not right for you right now, you can always come back and try again when you feel more ready. Again, it is a mindset thing. When you are ready you will do it and you will derive the benefits from it.

Now, I have a request and a favor to ask of you. Would you please consider giving this book a review on Amazon? I would be very grateful and appreciative.

Thank you kindly.

* * *

11

Resources

Image Credits:

- Cover Photo by Olia Danilevich/ Pexels
- Chapter 1: Designed by vectorpocket / Freepik
- Chapter 2: **Image** by **rawpixel.com**
- Chapter 3: *Designed by vectorpocket / Freepik*
- Chapter 4: *Designed by vectorpocket / Freepik*
- Chapter 5: *Designed by Mixkit*
- Chapter 6: Image by studio4rt on Freepik
- Chapter 7: *Image by studio4rt on Freepik*
- Chapter 8: Image by Freepik
- Chapter 9: Design by mixkit
- Chapter 10: Image by Freepik

Citations:

Engert, V., Klimecki, O., & Kanske, P. (2023). **Spreading positive change: Societal benefits of meditation.** *Frontiers in Psychiatry, 14.* https://doi.org/10.3389/fpsyt.2023.1038051

How Meditation Brings World Peace – *EOC Institute.* (n.d.). https://e ocinstitute.org/meditation/meditation-and-world-peace

İzzetoğlu, M., Shewokis, P. A., Tsai, K., Dantoin, P., Sparango, K., & Min, K. (2020). **Short-Term effects of meditation on sustained attention as measured by FNIRS.** *Brain Sciences, 10*(9), 608. https://d oi.org/10.3390/brainsci10090608

Mag, S. Y. (2020). **The Benefits Of Meditating With Headphones** — SF YOGA MAG. *SF YOGA MAG.* https://www.sfyogamagazine.com /blog/2020/10/11/the-benefits-of-meditating-with-headphones

Majsiak, B. (2022, June 23). *A beginner's guide to breath work practices.* EverydayHealth.com. https://www.everydayhealth.com/alte rnative-health/living-with/ways-practice-breath-focused-meditation

Meditation: A simple, fast way to reduce stress. (2022, April 29). Mayo Clinic. https://www.mayoclinic.org/tests-procedures/meditatio n/in-depth/meditation/art-20045858

Pura Rasa - Guided Meditations. (2017, February 12). *Stress Relief Guided Meditation, Deep Peace And Grounding*[Video]. YouTube.

Reflect. (2023, May 21). 12 **Long-Term effects of Meditation on the Brain.** *Reflect.* https://www.meetreflect.com/blog/meditation-eff ect-brain/

Sandra Rolus. (2019, June 25). *Ho'oponopono for Self love & Radical Forgiveness* [Video]. YouTube.

The Art of Living. (2023, May 25). **The scientific benefits of meditation: head to heart, body to mind.** *Art Of Living (United States).* https://www.artofliving.org/us-en/meditation/benefits/benefi ts-of-meditation

The Mindful Movement. (2020, February 26). *Sleep Meditation for new beginnings and habit change | Deep sleep | Mindful Movement* [Video]. YouTube.

RESOURCES

* * *

About the Author

Leslie R. Herman was born and raised on the city line of New York City — more suburbs than city, but NYC nonetheless. She's a city girl with a deep love for nature and being outdoors. Living in Wales for four decades reinforced her love of small places where nature is abundant and never very far away, and she currently resides in western North Carolina, inside the Pisgah National Forest. When she is not swimming, Leslie is writing, meditating, shopping, cooking or eating, those being her greatest pleasures. She is inspired by the weather, the radio, and the Welsh anthropologist, Elaine Morgan. Leslie believes that while words and pictures are incredibly powerful, attention to our other senses is vital, and she is involved in sensory communications with a focus on listening. As a communicator she bears a huge responsibility to keep expanding her perspectives.

You can connect with me on:
 https://www.facebook.com/groups/1491000371266232

Printed in Great Britain
by Amazon

30057002R00030